Contents

	Foreword	2
1.	A dangerous word	3/4/5
	Focus 1 I am not creative	6
2.	Why promote creativity?	7/8
3.	Broadening our definition of creativity	9
4.	Democratising creativity	10/11
	Focus 2 The artist and the judge	12
5.	Creativity doesn't just happen	13/14/15
	Focus 3 Encouraging spontaneity	16
6.	Develop a 'could be' attitude	17/18/19
7.	Slow your hare brain	20
8.	Change the way you see the world	21/22
9.	Rethink your thinking	23/24/25
	Focus 4 The creative process	26
10.	Are schools promoting creativity?	27/28
11.	The implications for teachers	29/30
	Focus 5 Fostering our own creativity	31
12.	The implications for school leadership	32/33
13.	The implications for educational reform	34
	References and further reading	35/36

Foreword

This is one of a series of occasional papers published by Learning Unlimited, and now collected in a series under the general title. 'The Learning Teacher'. It continues the original purpose which is to keep teachers up-to-date with what we know about how children and young people learn and how effective teachers teach.

A doctor who failed to keep up-to-date with medical developments over the past twenty years would have a quiet surgery. Yet in education, many teachers have now been in post for longer than that without receiving similar opportunities to update their knowledge about learning and teaching.

These titles summarise our best understandings to date about how we learn and how best to help other people learn. We still have a lot to discover but our knowledge is rapidly growing thanks to advances in neurology, psychology and, not least, good classroom practice.

At the end of a busy day, most teachers have neither time nor energy to read lengthy academic texts. So the papers in The Learning Teacher series are short, readable and comprehensive: they 'do the reading for you' and those who want to know more are directed to further reading at the end.

This is one of three titles in the series focusing on the cognitive side of learning. The other two are 'Learning to Think' and 'Teaching for Understanding', which focus mainly on what is variously described as analytical, critical or 'hard' thinking. They discuss the value of such thinking and how teachers and schools can improve the ways in which they help students to develop analytical thinking and the kind of understandings it can lead to.

In contrast, this title looks at how teachers, schools and the education system as a whole can better foster creative thinking. This has sometimes been described as 'soft' rather than 'hard' thinking but we now recognize that creative thinking involves both hard and soft thinking and this is one aspect of creativity which is discussed here.

One person who read the earlier drafts of the text asked me to consider the extent to which I had written and presented my thinking about creativity in a creative way. As the sub-title suggests, I have taken a hard analytical look at creativity itself and how we can better develop it in ourselves and foster it in the young people we teach. That's partly because of the way I come to writing about learning and teaching but also because I want to reach people who do not consider themselves to be creative or good at soft thinking. If you are such a person, I hope you find that this hard look at creativity will not only persuade you of the need to soften up your thinking but help you to do so. Such is one of the many paradoxes of creativity.

I am grateful to Robin Lloyd Jones, Alison Waugh, Ian Barr and Hilda De Felice for comments on the first draft of this paper. My thanks also to Eric Young and Liz Callaghan for the excellent job they did in editing and producing the paper.

Ian Smith, January 2006

1. A dangerous word

creative: artistic, clever, fertile, gifted, imaginative, ingenious, inspired, inventive, original, productive, stimulating, visionary.

Collins Shorter Thesaurus

"Creativity is a dangerous word that is often misused."

*Christopher Frayling,
Head of the Design Council, 2001*

Myths about creativity

Most people think they have a pretty clear idea about what 'creativity' is and what it is to 'be creative'. It seems so simple and obvious. But 'creativity' is an ambiguous term. It can be thought of as something that goes on in your head, ideas or objects that people produce, or a quality or characteristic someone possesses that makes her or him worthwhile.

Traditionally, it has been associated with the achievements of extraordinary individuals such as Mozart, Einstein and Leonardo Da Vinci. But it's also used in relation to the inventiveness and imagination that is well within the capacity of ordinary people. The idea that creative people are somehow special is only one of a number of myths about creativity.

Four big myths about creativity

Creativity only happens in certain areas of human activity. In school it's virtually the sole domain of the so called 'creative arts' and has very little part to play in subjects like science, technology or mathematics. In the world generally, it's about being a writer, a dancer or an artist. It has nothing to do with running a company, finding a fault in your central heating or bringing up a family on a low income.

The creative process just happens like a bolt from the blue. It's always inspirational, spontaneous and effortless. It's about 'letting go', about free expression and being uninhibited and it's nothing to do with hard work. It's also about doing your own thing: highly creative people are loners.

Creative people are somehow special. They are more intelligent than the rest of us, a bit different from the rest of us and maybe actually a bit strange or 'way-out' in some way. Creative geniuses are born, not made and creativity is some kind of mystical gift from the gods. If you don't possess it, you can't be creative.

All creative work is original. You have to start with an absolutely original idea of your own. Creative people do their own thing: they are loners. They do not work with others or use other people's thinking and ideas. That would be cheating.

Traditional studies reinforce these myths

Much work has been done over many years now to understand creativity by studying people who are considered to be 'geniuses' in the accepted use of the term. The danger is that this kind of work simply perpetuates the myth that creativity is about special people doing special things. The list below, collected from a range of sources, illustrates this.

1. A dangerous word

The characteristics of highly creative people

They have extensive experience and apprenticeship: no truly great creative contributions have come without at least ten years of intensive effort and preparation.

They know what works and what doesn't: they know what is original and what is not, what people like and dislike, what people admire and do not. But above all they are experts - they develop a strong expertise and a large base of knowledge in whatever field they are working.

They have imaginative thinking skills: they can see things in new ways, recognise patterns and make connections, look in opposite directions at the same time.

They are remarkably resilient and courageous: they have a 'venturesome personality', tolerate ambiguity and risk, do not suppress a problem but engage in 'creative worrying', persevere in overcoming obstacles and seek new experiences rather than following the pack.

They are fully engaged in and passionate about their work: they exhibit a strong desire to do something new and have a strong sense of their purpose and ultimate goals.

They are motivated primarily by the interest, engagement, satisfaction and challenge of the work itself: they are not distracted by external pressures such as deadlines, impressing people or making money.

They work hard and practice hard: they are painstaking, they revise endlessly to get close to their ideal.

They are extremely reflective about their activities: they think about how they use their time and the quality of their products.

They have almost always lived in their early years in a creative environment that nurtures and supports creative ideas: they are not lone geniuses; they were mentored, challenged and supported by other people; they are free from concern about social approval and too much external judgement and evaluation especially at the start of the process.

Main Sources: Rothenberg (1990), Myers (1995), Csiksentmihalyi (1996), Cropley (2001), Damasio (2001)

Creativity as an inherent, developable skill

When you read a list like this, it is hardly surprising that so many people believe that they are not creative *(see Focus 1)*. Ironically, the research revealed that no specific personality type is associated with outstanding creativity and that creative geniuses are not necessarily outstandingly intelligent in the common meaning of the word. What they do share is very strong motivation and an extraordinary capacity in their field, for example the manual proficiency required for music, facility with language required in literature or the use of abstract symbols in mathematics.

This exclusive attitude to creativity is what professionals in the field have been working hard to overturn. Alison Waugh (2003) believes that perception is moving away from the 'genius' model to a broader view that creative thinking is an inherent developable skill. She points out that, as long ago as 1954, Abraham Maslow talked about the difference between 'special talent creativity' and 'self-actualising creativity'.

I intend to look at this self-actualising creativity and at how we can help those who are not seen as unusually intelligent or talented to develop it.

1. A dangerous word

ARE YOUR LEARNERS SUFFERING FROM
locks on creativity?

1. A dangerous word

Focus 1

I am not creative

"Most individuals truly believe they are not creative. They let their greatest asset go undeveloped because of combined messages received from family, friends, schools, church, or people at work."

Land and Jarman (1992)

In 1990, Roger Von Oech, who wrote perhaps the most accessible book on creativity available, invented the term 'mental locks' to describe how our attitudes can get in the way of our creativity. He suggested that the locks can be opened in one of two ways. The first is to become aware of them, and then forget them temporarily when you are trying to generate new ideas. If that does not work, you need a 'whack on the side of the head' to dislodge the presuppositions that hold the locks in place.

However, our beliefs are not the only things that get in the way of creativity. Most commentators agree that the two most significant external locks on creativity are excess pressure and lack of time. Bearing this in mind I have taken the liberty of devising a list of school locks on creativity.

Mental locks on creativity	School locks on creativity
• The right answer	• Back to the basics
• That's not logical	• Cover the content
• Follow the rules	• Knowledge in boxes
• Be practical	• It's all in the head
• Play is frivolous	• Planning makes perfect
• That's not my area	• Every minute is important
• Avoid ambiguity	• Fun is frivolous
• Don't be foolish	• We're paid to teach
• To err is wrong	• Testing, testing, testing
• I am not creative	• Control above all

Source: Roger Von Oech
'A Whack on the Side of the Head'

2. Why promote creativity?

"Imagination is more important than knowledge." *Albert Einstein*

"The choice is stark for companies in the modern world: create or fail." *John Kao, 1997*

Creativity is not necessarily a good thing. We could argue that Hitler and Stalin were extremely creative. The people who brainwash suicide bombers are very creative and ingenious in persuading them that what they are doing is noble, while those who run Guantanamo Bay are also creative in their interrogation techniques. Whether creativity is a good thing or not depends on the use to which it is put and the beliefs and value systems on which it draws.

Having said that, we are gradually realising that creativity can be a force for good, not just for the economy, but for society as a whole and for individuals. The quote from Einstein above has become a commonplace.

Many stress the importance of creativity to the economy. On one level, people point to the importance of the creative industries. Sir Ken Robinson (2001) for example, thinks that, if we categorise advertising, architecture, arts and antiques, crafts, design, fashion, film, leisure software, music, performing arts, publishing, software and computer services, television and radio as the creative industries, then their contribution to the British economy in 1988 was around £6 billion a year. By 1998, the government reckoned it was £60 billion - a ten fold increase. Employment in these industries grew 34% in the same period against a background of almost no growth in the economy as a whole.

But, as Robinson himself recognises, this is not just about getting more people into jobs in the creative industries. In the knowledge economy, the capacities associated with creativity and ingenuity are needed in more and more jobs at all levels in both in the private and the public sector. The increased pressure of competition has led to a much greater emphasis on customer focus and working to achieve continuous improvement. So, people at all levels need to take the initiative in decision making and deal with ambiguity and paradox rather than waiting to be told or hiding behind rules and procedures.

Thinking and creating together

In the modern world, the skills and qualities we associate with creativity and ingenuity are not only required for economic competitiveness but to help us to work together more effectively. Andy Hargreaves (2003) has pointed out that schools now operate in a global world, a knowledge economy and a knowledge society. He argues that creative thinking is needed in a participative democracy, in communities and at a personal level and suggests that knowledge society schools have to create these qualities, otherwise their people and their nations will be left behind.

Hargreaves argues that many of the problems facing us all in the modern world (poverty, global warming, terrorism, binge drinking, drug addiction and the break-up of traditional families) cannot be solved by simply searching for the cause and seeking to remove it. Instead, there is a need, as Edward de Bono puts it, 'to design new ways forward'.

Alison Waugh (2002) points out that creativity in the Western world is often thought of as an individual process while in Japan it is seen as collaborative. The Japanese approach to creativity is superficially similar to the Western but with some crucial differences: it uses existing material, it is a group not an individual activity and it is informed at all points of the process by shared core values. Waugh notes that teams all over the world use the Japanese process model of creativity to solve problems and generate ideas.

1. Why promote creativity

Personal creativity

Coming up with new ideas and solving everyday problems *(see pages x and y)* is also extremely important in our personal lives. It plays a critically important part in personal learning and development. It builds self confidence and self esteem. It is challenging and it is fun.

Creativity in school

Few people now argue with the importance of creativity but, more and more, we are coming to recognise that our education system is struggling to foster creativity despite encouragement from government *(see Focus 1: School locks on creativity).*

In recent years, two major reports have been published on the state of creativity in schools in the UK. The first, entitled 'All Our Futures: Creativity, Culture and Education', was produced in 1999 by the National Advisory Committee on Creative and Cultural Education in England and Wales. The second, 'Creativity in Education', was published by Learning and Teaching Scotland in 2001. Both reports took a very similar line. They both sought to define creativity, emphasise its social and economic importance and assure us that it can be fostered and developed. They were critical of the school system's inability to promote and develop creativity and made a range of recommendations as to what should be done. Ken Robinson, the author of All Our Futures, received a knighthood but was reported as saying that he believes the report was sidelined. He now works in California. At best, the Scottish Executive has paid lip service to 'Creativity in Education'.

Sir Ken Robinson recently published a book on creativity and lectures widely on it. He is not downhearted at the response to the 'All Our Futures' report, but is critical of politicians. He suggests that they 'just don't get' why creativity is so important in our society, or that they think it's some kind of throwback to the woolly progressivism of the 1960s personified by figures like Piaget. This may well be part of the reason for the narrow view we take of what constitutes achievement in our schools, but I don't think it is the only factor.

I want to go beyond these two reports. Both spent too much time exhorting teachers and schools to foster creative thinking more effectively and not enough time offering practical ways to do this. My main aim is to provide a much more detailed overview of the available practical advice on how to develop your creativity and help other people develop their creativity.

Schools will help foster creativity only by showing young people that they are creative, but first I want to go further than either of these reports did by redefining what we mean by creativity and, even more importantly, how we think we become creative.

We need to bridge the gap between the need for creativity in the real world and the belief shared by most people that they are not creative. We also need to challenge directly negative beliefs about what creativity is and how we become creative and these are the topics of the next two sections.

3. Broadening our definition of creativity

"I define creativity as the entire process by which ideas are generated, developed and transformed into value. It comprises what people commonly mean by innovation and entrepreneurship." *John Kao, 1997*

It would be good if we could just scrap the word 'creativity' - it has become such a misunderstood concept. Edward De Bono (1970) recognised this and wrote about 'lateral thinking' as 'a deliberate process of moving sideways from established ways of looking at things to find new ways'. The term has stuck and you will find it in the dictionary, but it has not replaced creativity. So the strategy must be not how we replace creativity but how we redefine the concept. I think we need to do this in two related ways – by broadening it and by democratising it.

We can broaden the concept of creativity firstly by recognising that it is not about coming up with big ideas, but finding practical solutions to everyday problems and then applying them or making them work in the real world. Everything around us – our houses, our cities, our medical services, our transport and communication systems - were built and are being developed by practical people who know how to get into a creative frame of mind.

This means bringing together the concepts of creativity, inventiveness, entrepreneurship and enterprise so often treated separately in schools. It also means putting a greater emphasis on practical thinking and practical subjects so often under-rated in schools.

- **Creativity** is about the generation of ideas, usually new ideas (it is mostly a divergent, non-evaluative process)

- **Ingenuity** is about the successful exploitation of ideas, including old ideas that are useful (it is mostly a convergent, evaluative process)

Secondly we can broaden our definition of creativity by acccepting that it is not an extraordinary, special one-off event but an everyday activity which we are all good at. Look at the activities below, rethink how creative you are as a person and add to the list. We greatly underestimate the importance of creativity and inventiveness at a personal level and the extent to which it is needed in a wide range of everyday tasks and activities. Some of the examples I have listed below illustrate that creative thinking is not only closely linked to practical thinking but also to emotional thinking or what has come to be known as emotional intelligence.

Examples of ordinary everyday creativity

- Creating humour out of any situation no matter how bad
- Keeping a fractious child happy
- Finding a way of interesting a class in a topic they find boring
- Planning a trip which all the family will enjoy
- Selecting an original and imaginative gift that costs next to nothing
- Helping two people to resolve a conflict

4. Democratising creativity

We are all hard-wired to be creative

"The genius creates good ideas because we all create new ideas: that is what our minds are for." *Steven Pinker, 2002*

We also need to redefine creativity by democratising it. This is less about what we think creativity is than about our beliefs on how we become creative and how creative we are as individuals. We need to undermine the 'I am not creative' mentality by recognising that we are all capable of being creative and thinking creatively. But we also have to recognise that this does not make us all geniuses. Indeed, we need to separate the words creative and genius in our minds.

Psychologists have been making a case for inborn creativity for many years. As early as 1957, Abraham Maslow talked about 'primary creativeness'. It comes out of the unconscious, and is the "source of new discoveries, of real novelty, which departs from what exists". There is a growing body of evidence to support Steven Pinker's more recent research. For instance, Stanley Greenspan (1997) suggests that the potential for invention and creativity appears at a very young age. Like Pinker, he believes we are genetically disposed to be creative.

Leaving available scientific evidence aside, I think most of us would accept from our own experience that young children typically display more of the qualities that are associated with creativity than adults. Indeed I shall argue later that adults need to rediscover their own childhood if they are to be more creative. Children are inquisitive, have great imagination and fantasies which are an important part of their play. They explore, ask questions and are unafraid of being ridiculed. In fact you cannot stop them asking questions. A study quoted by George Land (1992) claimed that, on average, they ask 125 each day compared with an adult's 6! I have not been able to track that study down either but I believe it.

Does this mean that we are all potentially 'creative geniuses'?

The answer is no. But I think it's worth asking this question and answering it because many people make great claims about our potential for creative genius based on what appears to me to be very flimsy evidence. For example, Land (1992) claimed that his research showed that "the vast majority of small children are creative geniuses". He gave eight tests of divergent thinking to 1600 children in the early days of the Headstart programme. He gave the same tests to these children over several years. And the results were that when they were 3-5 years of age, 98% came out in the 'genius' category and when they were 10 years old, 32% came out in the 'genius' category. He gave two thousand adults the same tests and only 2% scored at the 'genius' level.

I've not been able to find out where his research is published, but, despite the fact I believe passionately in people's potential, I think it's counterproductive to overemphasise the extent to which all children and indeed all of us are potentially 'creative geniuses'. That leads people to think that they are being asked to believe that if any one of us gets the right upbringing, is motivated enough and works hard enough, we could all be Einsteins, Mozarts or Shakespeares, which in turn leads to cynicism. Common sense, never mind science, refutes the idea and it does not help us to democratise creativity and leave the 'I am not creative' belief behind.

4. Democratising creativity

WORKING WITH THE
artist and
the judge.

4. Democratising creativity

Focus 2

The artist and the judge

"Each one of you has an 'artist' and a 'judge' inside you. You need them both to be creative, but avoid bringing your judge in before your artist has had a chance to do her job." *Roger Von Oech, 1990*

"The truth is that creative people appreciate controls and even rely on them." *John Kao, 1997*

"Generating ideas, solving problems, taking decisions involves being both analytical and creative. It involves divergent or 'soft' thinking, taking risks with your thinking in ways that may defy logic and appear foolish or absurd to other people. It frequently involves the suspension of critical or 'hard' thinking to allow new ideas to develop, new associations to form or new responses to emerge in your mind." *Windy Dryden, 1994*

It's important to know when each is not appropriate. The trick is to know when each is useful and to have the courage to use soft thinking in the first place. It means you need to be free to have a lot of bad or 'off-the-wall' ideas and not dismiss them right away. But that's not the same as being free to implement the bad idea and therefore fail. The 'judge' needs to intervene before that happens.

Hard
- Certain
- Close down
- One right answer
- Exact
- Fast
- Looking
- Black and white
- Analysis
- Logic
- Differences and categories
- Rational
- Precise
- Serious
- Focused
- Familiar

Soft
- Doubtful
- Open up
- Many right answers
- Approximate
- Slow
- Waiting
- Many shades of grey to say nothing of orange purple etc
- Hunches
- Intuition
- Similarities and connections
- Dreamy
- Woolly
- Playful
- Diffuse
- New

5. Creativity doesn't just happen

So far, I have tried to define the slippery concept of creativity and what we know about it. I've suggested that it is really important for our economy and our society and for us as individuals. I've argued strongly that it is not simply in-born, that we are all creative, that we can learn to be more creative and we can improve our ability to come up with ideas.

Now we arrive at the two central questions. Firstly, how do we become better soft, lateral or out-of-the-box thinkers? How do we develop what Keats called 'negative capability', the "ability to remain in uncertainties, mysteries, doubts, without any irritable reaching after fact or reason"? Secondly, how can we foster creativity and ingenuity in other people, especially when they believe that they are not creative or ingenious?

There's certainly no shortage of advice about. Go to the business section or the self-help section of your local bookshop and you will find there is a bewildering range of titles on the subject. The problem is trying to make sense of it all, especially when some of the advice seems conflicting. I will try to do that in the following pages. Before we go into detail however, we need to focus on some key points about fostering creativity and ingenuity.

Fostering creativity is not about simply releasing our natural potential

"Espousing the idea that everyone is naturally creative, but just becomes inhibited as they grow up and all we have to do is remove these inhibitions and we will unlock natural creativity is a myth." *Edward De Bono, 1992*

In the last section we looked at children's natural capacity for creativity. What we did not explore was the nature of children's creativity or why and how it differs from adults' creativity. Vygotsky suggested that young children's creativity is 'less rich' than that of adults because of their limited knowledge base and less complex cognitions. It also tends to be more subjective than adult creativity. Children tend to create for themselves and adults create both for themselves and for the outside world. De Bono suggested that the creativity of young children comes from innocence. If you don't know the usual approach, the usual solution, the usual concepts involved, then you may come up with a fresh approach.

Also I think we can recognise that young children's creativity comes from their lack of knowledge and awareness of the world - a lack that does not faze them. They are uninhibited and it may well be that, as we grow older, the inhibitions develop and creativity is stifled. That leads a lot of people to suggest that we should prevent these inhibitions occurring and simply let young people unleash their natural creativity. De Bono has challenged this view as dangerous and wrong headed, pointing out that it is not easy to remain ignorant and innocent as we grow up. Neither is it desirable!

5. Creativity doesn't just happen

Creativity is a skill that needs to be developed

"We really need to stop considering thinking as simply 'intelligence in action' and think of it as a skill that can be developed by everyone." *Edward De Bono, 1982*

It's easier to argue that to foster creativity in adults you need to 'unblock' them, 'defrost' them or get them to 'chill out'. De Bono believes that this may make people slightly more creative but not much. He thinks that to foster creativity effectively we have to consciously and conscientiously develop specific thinking techniques which older children and adults may find difficult.

De Bono believes that, although the human brain is capable of great creativity and ingenuity, it is not designed for this first and foremost. He places great importance on perception, which he thinks has been undervalued by psychologists. He points out that perception is crucial for the brain's main purpose of enabling us to survive and cope.
To do this, it forms patterns from the world around us and then sticks to those patterns. This is how perception works and life would be totally impossible were it otherwise.

To cut across established patterns to produce new ideas is not what the brain is designed to do. That is why we need to use tools to shock or force the brain to think laterally. De Bono argues that, as we grow older, it is more difficult to think laterally because the patterns become so well established and comfortable. The wide range of techniques that De Bono has developed over many years are mostly designed to help us do this.

De Bono thinks that, to become more creative, it is not enough to work on your attitude *(section 7)*, it is not enough to slow down your mind or alter your mental state *(section 8)*, it is not enough even to understand the strategies you need to follow. You need to actually use tools and techniques systematically and deliberately *(sections 9 and 10)*. As De Bono says, this is much more reliable and when he does use them himself, he usually surprises himself with an idea.

Creativity involves both 'hard' and 'soft' thinking

In my view, this is by far the most important point now being made about the creative process. So-called 'hard' thinking which requires what has traditionally been thought of as academic intelligence is not the most crucial element in creativity or ingenuity and can even get in the way. But the idea that creative people are right brained, exclusively 'soft thinkers' has been abandoned in favour of the view that it involves the whole brain, a mixture of 'hard' and 'soft' thinking
(see Focus 4).

Being creative involves making judgements and evaluating but the real skill is in knowing when to do that and not rushing to judgement. Guy Claxton (1996) has even described creativity as thinking less and he points out that, "The brain is built to linger as well as rush and sometimes slow browsing leads to better answers". The key point is to give soft thinking or what De Bono calls lateral thinking a chance. That often means 'stopping' and giving yourself a 'whack on the side of the head' in some way.

I think Arthur Cropley (2001) has described this better than most. He says that creative people manage to 'integrate opposites' and identifies eight kinds of opposites that they are able to bring together. According to Cropley, to be creative you need to be able to integrate these opposites and to have what he has called a balanced or 'paradoxical personality'.

5. Creativity doesn't just happen

Creativity is closely linked to the emotions and how you feel about yourself

> "Though we don't want to admit it, in the end, all decisions are emotional." *Edward De Bono*

You will have recognised by now that I believe that Edward de Bono has contributed more than anyone else to our understanding of creativity and how to promote it. However, when it comes to the role of emotions in creativity, I think his ideas are flawed. He recognises that all decisions are emotional but suggests that we need to engage our emotions at the end of our thinking rather than at the start. His mantra, 'stop and think' is mainly about this: don't go with your gut feeling until you have thought about it.

I don't believe this is easy advice to follow and often it is not desirable. Emotions certainly cannot be separated from thinking. It is better to take Carl Jung's line and see feeling as a rational process.

So you can never take the red hat off *(see Focus 5)* and some people have a natural preference to use feelings first (see Different in Similar Ways).

Other titles in this series focus on the role of the emotions in learning, but here it is worth mentioning the work of American child psychiatrist, Stanley Greenspan (1997) He has looked at the way that the emotions and intelligence interact in babies and very young children. He concluded that emotional experience is necessary for the acquisition of cognitive skills and claims that the emotions make all creative thought possible. I believe that is true for adults as well as babies.

You can foster creativity in others but you can't foist it on them

> "You don't teach creativity, you teach people to let themselves be creative." *Julia Cameron, 1994*

> "It is possible to turn unimaginative people into imaginative people at a moment's notice." *Keith Johnstone, 1981*

This is related to the first point in this section which discussed the extent to which creativity and ingenuity can simply be 'released'. There is potential for confusion here and the advice can be seen as conflicting. Two examples illustrate this.

Julia Cameron is a well respected author whose best known work, 'The Artist's Way', is mainly about opening yourself to your own latent creativity. She does not advocate conscious techniques such as those outlined in sections 9 and 10 but ideas that "bring you into contact with your inner power". These ideas take time.

In contrast Keith Johnstone, a renowned specialist in teaching improvisation to actors, claims he can help people tap into their imaginations at a moment's notice *(see Focus 5)*.

Both Julia Cameron and Keith Johnstone's techniques are effective. You cannot make someone creative or ingenious, but skillful facilitators can help other people to get ideas more quickly than they ever imagined they could by using techniques which help them tap into their unconscious mind more systematically and, as Julia Cameron puts it, 'get ideas out' and 'let ideas in'. The next four sections look at three broad strategies we can use to foster creativity in ourselves and in others. They involve deliberately fostering the disposition to be creative, actively taking steps to slow down your thinking and using specific thinking techniques.

5. Creativity doesn't just happen

Focus 3

Encouraging spontaneity

The examples in Keith Johnstone's classic text 'Impro' illustrate in very practical terms ideas that can help people to unblock and produce ideas in a much wider range of contexts. This page gives an example of encouraging spontaneity in the specialist, creative area of drama.

In this case, the exercise is not about helping students to relax but is very directive, even confrontational. But it is not about giving students ideas: it is about fostering not foisting. In the first example, Johnstone explores a technique that drama teachers regularly use with school students.

If I say to a student, 'Imagine a box and tell me what you think is in it', uninvited answers may well spring to mind. It could be a body. If articulated, people might laugh or think the student is insane or callous. It could be hundreds of toilet rolls, but the student doesn't want to appear preoccupied with excretion. So finally, after a pause of perhaps two seconds, he says 'old clothes' or 'it's empty'.

I say to another student 'name some objects'.

She tenses up. 'Er...pebble...beach...cliff...er...er'.

'Have you any idea why you have blocked?' I ask.

'I just keep thinking of pebble'.

'Then say it. Say whatever occurs to you. It doesn't need to be original.'

Normally, the mind does not even know it is rejecting the first answers and they do not go into the long term memory. So, if I didn't ask the student immediately, she would deny she was substituting better words. Teaching students to accept the first idea makes them seem much more inventive.

I sometimes shock students who have been trained by strict 'method' teachers in the following way:

'Be sad,' I say.

'What do you mean, be sad?'

'Just be sad. See what happens.'

'But what is my motivation?'

'Just be sad. Start to weep and you will know what has upset you.'

(The student decides to humour me.)

'That isn't sad. You're just pretending.'

'You asked me to pretend.'

'Raise your arm. Now, why are you raising it?'

'You asked me to.'

'Yes, but why might you have raised your arm?'

'To hold onto a strap on the Tube.'

'Then, that's why you raised your arm.'

'But I could have given any reason.'

'Of course.'

'But I don't have time to choose the best reason.'

'Don't choose anything. Trust your mind. Take the first idea it gives to you. Now try to be sad again. Hold your face in a sad position, fight back the tears. Be unhappier. More. More. Now tell me why you're in this state.'

'My child died.'

'Did you think that up?'

'I just knew.'

'There you are then.'

Source: Keith Johnstone 'Impro'

6. Develop a 'could-be' attitude

Many authors talk about the 'disposition' that some people seem to have to be creative and ingenious, of developing a creative 'attitude' or of fostering 'habits' or 'states of mind' that lead you to be more creative and ingenious. This section describes what a 'could be' attitude might look like and suggests six ways to foster it in yourself and to help other people develop it.

"Expect the unexpected or you won't find it." *Roger Von Oech, 2001*

1. Delete 'I am not creative'

If you think that there is only one solution to every problem and that you are not good at solving problems or coming up with ideas, then you will never realise your potential for creativity or ingenuity. Creative people don't just believe, but know that ideas are 'in the air'. They are all around us, and for every problem there is always another idea, another solution. They also know that they will find them. The trouble is that too many people believe that when faced with a problem there is only one right solution and that they will never find that solution because they 'never get ideas'. Delete the 'I am not creative' attitude and become what Jack Foster (1996) calls 'ideas prone'.

"If you don't know where you are going, any road will take you there." *Lewis Carroll*

2. Define what you want

If you set your mind on getting ideas, you will come up with them, but it helps to have a sense of purpose, to define what you want. Most highly creative people find something to be creative or ingenious about. This might be something they want to dedicate their entire life to, like Franz Schubert, who said, "I am in the world for the purpose of composing". Or it might simply be a specific problem they want to solve, like Henry Ford, whose problem was how to mass produce motor cars.

Developing your true sense of purpose in life or defining a problem correctly is not so much about finding the right answers, but asking the right questions. These might be fundamental questions such as what you really, really want out of life. What do you enjoy doing? Or they might be about making a fundamental shift in a very basic question from 'how do we get the people to the work?' to 'how do we get the work to the people?'

"It is difficult to have creativity without humour, to have ideas without fun and to have performance without enjoyment." *Jack Foster, 1996*

3. Have fun: play with ideas

If you want to be creative, recognise that you cannot be serious, at least not all the time. Serious people have fewer ideas. Having fun unleashes creativity and ingenuity. From Arthur Koestler to Edward de Bono, people who have written on creativity have emphasized how closely creative thinking is linked to humour and how humour acts as a stimulus for creativity and ingenuity. This involves rediscovering the child within. Children are much better at fun, fantasy and wonderment than adults. They break the rules because they don't know they exist. They constantly see new relationships between seemingly unrelated things: they study ordinary things intently and have a sense of wonder about what adults take for granted.

6. Develop a 'could-be' attitude

> "Doubt is an uncomfortable position but certainty is a ridiculous one." *Voltaire*

4. Practise not knowing

We need to learn to tolerate ambiguity. Children don't just play, they puzzle. They have to be comfortable about not knowing and are not afraid to ask questions when they don't know or understand. Adults are less happy about this. We often pretend we understand when we don't. We may ask one question for clarification but then not ask a second if we still don't understand. Young children have the confidence to ask, ask and ask. So work at not knowing. Practise saying, 'I don't know'. Try to do this three times a day if you can. This is good but risky for all of us, especially teachers. To begin with, you can reduce the risk by choosing situations where you find it easiest and then gravitate to more challenging places (e.g. at home, then the staffroom, then classroom – or the other way round!)

> "I am neither especially clever, nor especially gifted. I am only very, very curious." *Albert Einstein*

5. Be very, very curious

This is yet another characteristic of young children. They are fantastically curious about the world and seek out new experiences. Adults are less inclined to do so. We are locked into our routines, happy with the familiar. Von Oech (2001) asks us to beware of routines, pointing out that they are "the boon and the bane of our existence". Robert Wiseman (2004) suggests, "The less routine, the more life". He observes that scientists have studied the psychology of curiosity for over a century and have devised a wide variety of tests to measure the degree to which people are curious about the world. Wiseman's research has shown that these people also experience more lucky breaks than others. Foster points out that creative and ingenious people avoid getting in a rut, and by doing so they 'get more inputs'. Be open to new ideas, to new experiences and to new ways of looking at things. Bring something new into your life or do something differently, each day, each week and each year. This is especially important if you are a creature of routine and you have worked in the same place for a long period of time.

> "Do not fear mistakes – there are none." *Miles Davis*

6. Face your fears

Of course, there are situations when it is potentially catastrophic to make a mistake – when you are landing a plane, for instance! But the logic of previous sections tells us that creativity and ingenuity require not only confidence and desire, but the courage to make mistakes. We live in a culture that is addicted to certainty. It doesn't encourage playfulness, uncertainty or mistakes. In the adult world, there is a pressure to come up with the right answer, to be certain about things, to eliminate doubt. This is particularly true of people in positions of power and responsibility. The last thing a politician can say in response to an interviewer's question is "I don't know". And, of course, the teacher is always expected to know the right answer. Not to know suggests powerlessness, lack of control, even weakness. Face your fears one at a time, from the least to the most frightening. Instead of asking, "What will people think of me?", ask yourself, "Does that really matter?" Instead of asking yourself, "What if I fail?", ask yourself, "What if I succeed?"

6. Develop a 'could-be' attitude

> "Conversation doesn't just reshuffle the cards: it creates new cards." *Theodore Zeldin*

7. Be sociable sometimes

De Bono (1992) says that, because brainstorming has been the traditional approach to deliberate creative thinking, people tend to assume that creative thinking must be a group process. In his experience, the opposite is the case. Individuals on their own produce far more ideas and a wider range of ideas than when they are working in a group. He does not deny that the social aspects of the group have value and recognises that it does require a lot of discipline to work creatively on your own.

Claxton and Lucas (2004) believe that we need to be sociable sometimes and that creativity and ingenuity flourish on a diet of both being alone and being sociable. Sometimes we need the door open and sometimes we need it shut.

We need to talk to people about our ideas along the way. Michalko tells us that, when researching the lives of famous scientists, the physicist, David Bohm, found out that huge breakthroughs came from simple direct conversations where there was genuine dialogue and the freedom to discuss without risk.

Waugh (2002) argues that these are both Western views which see creativity as mainly an individual act, whereas in other cultures, like Japan, creativity is primarily a collective activity. She stresses the need to be collective and would emphasise the importance of getting the best balance between the personal and the collective for everyone in a group and for the group as a whole.

> "Nothing is ever accomplished without enthusiasm. And the more enthusiasm the better." *Ralph Waldo Emerson*

8. Go for it

People who succeed in any field through their creativity, 'go for it' in two senses. Firstly they practise or work hard. Michelangelo's comment on this is well known: "If they knew how hard I have to work to achieve my mastery they would not think it so wonderful." Artists and entrepreneurs alike find what they want to do and immerse themselves in it. They are also patient and persistent, prepared to defer gratification. They don't expect to be an overnight success.

Secondly, they 'go for it' in the sense that they are pro-active. They don't sit around waiting for something to happen. Anyone who simply waits for an idea to come has a long wait coming. Knaus (1998) noted that creativity is not something that is just on tap: "You can't just wait for moments of inspiration to come while suffering from a lack of accomplishment. You are more likely to have creative moments if you 'force yourself' to be creative. Only then will you avoid the eternal plight of the frustrated artist."

Robert Graves wrote 'I Claudius' in a matter of weeks to pay outstanding bills. Mascagni wrote the Intermezzo to Cavaleria Rusticana overnight as he was five minutes short for the opening performance the next day. It is now his most famous piece. Foster quotes the journalist, Andy Rooney: "If I have a deadline for a column or a television script, I sit down at my typewriter and damn well have an idea. There's nothing magical about the process". As Foster puts it, "deadlines spur you on to something. Give yourself one."

Main sources: Steve Bowkett (1997)
Guy Claxton and Bill Lucas (2004), Jack Foster (1996)

7. Slow your hare brain

"The creative act depends on unconscious resources which require a relaxing of controls for us to access."

Arthur Koestler, 1964

"Saturate your mind with your subject, then wait."

Lloyd Morgan, 1930

In the last section, we stressed the importance of going for it. By this we meant being pro-active, working hard and to deadlines. But, as we have already noted (Focus 4), one of the paradoxes about creativity and ingenuity is that, although they involve hard work and effort, they also involve relaxing and letting go. This concept has a long and distinguished pedigree in psychology. Arthur Koestler (1964) illustrated this paradox by referring to Picasso ("I do not seek, I find") and Thomas Edison ("Creativity is 99% perspiration and 1% inspiration").

Most creative revelations come because we have worked at a problem but they also only appear after we have stopped the hard work and let go of the struggle to come to a solution. Koestler talked about long donkey work followed by the brief flash of insight. So they tend to come when we are not trying too hard, when our minds are involved in some completely unrelated activity or after a good night's sleep, when we are relaxed but alert. This is because the brain continues to work on a problem once it has been supplied with the necessary raw materials and has a chance to process them in the unconscious mind. It's what has been described as 'mental fermentation' or 'incubation'.

For many people, it's not the hard work that is difficult, but the waiting. We need to develop techniques which allow us to alter our state of mind, to slow down our hare brain and give our tortoise mind a chance, as Guy Claxton (1998) suggested in the title of one of his books. He talked about the need for us to relax, daydream, contemplate and mull over what we have already learned if we are to foster creativity and ingenuity. This is what Kao (1997) calls using your 'beginner's mind' and the Scottish mathematician, James Clark Maxwell, called 'the perfectly conscious unconscious'.

Foster (1996) talks about the need to forget about an idea once you have searched for it and not found it. Often he points out there is not time to do this, but for him the weight of evidence suggests that when you are having trouble solving a problem or coming up with an idea, forgetting about it is as essential as searching for it. A wide range of highly successful people have claimed that their best ideas have come to them not when they were searching for them. For example, Einstein said his best ideas came to him when he was shaving.

Foster says relaxing is not about vegetating by watching sitcoms on TV. For him, mental relaxation is overrated and it might be counterproductive, for it stops momentum and shuts down the effort it takes to look at things hard enough to recognize similarities, connections and relationships. He says forgetting is about shifting gears and that, when you forget about one thing, it can be helpful to start working on another.

While he plays down the importance of relaxation, Foster does suggest that meditation can help generate ideas. Claxton and Lucas openly advocate relaxation techniques and motivation. Meditation and relaxation techniques are not mysterious, new nor particularly difficult. They help us to silence our chattering mind and our internal critic, to tackle mental stress and physical tension which feed off each other and, once at a certain level, cause our brain to miss the bigger picture and make it far less able to see the world in new and original ways.

8. Change the way you see the world

> "85% of thinking is a matter of perception. Most faults in thinking are not faults in logic, but faults in perception. Perception is the basis of wisdom."
> *Edward De Bono, 1992*

> "Originality is simply a fresh pair of eyes."
> *Woodrow Wilson*

Most writers on creativity agree that much of creativity and ingenuity is about improving perception, going beyond the obvious and seeing what no-one else is seeing. Claxton and Lucas tell us that scientists have recently discovered that our brains are hard-wired to arrive at preconceptions (to jump to conclusions) that allow us to make the strange familiar. This helped our ancestors to survive in a hostile world and, in many ways, it still makes good sense to us today. Indeed, it allows us to cope with all the stimuli that the modern world throws at us. The problem is that our brains become focused on what we expect to see. We see what we look for. We jump to conclusions about what things are and put them into categories. We miss things that are obvious and unexpected. In looking for solutions, we dig deeper in the same hole. As De Bono put it, 'the main purpose of the brain is to be brilliantly uncreative'.

> "The hardest thing to see is what is right in front of your eyes."
> *Goethe*

Learn how to see

One of the main ways in which we can train ourselves to be more creative is to use strategies that will switch our brains off auto-pilot and see beyond the non-obvious. A whole range of techniques are available. De Bono's thinking tools (see below) are all about helping us to heighten our perception to avoid impulsivity, defer judgement and remove the need to be right or get a quick answer. As De Bono says, they are mainly designed to help us **stop then think.** As Fisher (1995) points out, these are particularly useful techniques to use openly and systematically with young children who are egocentric. But adults are not immune to egocentricity!

- **PMI: Plus, Minus and Interesting** is a way of generating thinking about the different aspects of an idea or an action. What would be the plus and minus and interesting consequences?
- **CAF: Consider all Factors** is a technique for generating ideas and increasing the breadth of perception, for example: what makes a good teacher?
- **C & S: Consequences and Sequel** helps people to speculate on and predict the consequences of their actions
- **AGO: Aims, Goals and Objectives** is about why you are doing something: what is the purpose? What are you hoping to achieve?
- **FIP: First Important Priorities** is a way of directing attention towards priorities, for example: which are the most important factors in being a good teacher?
- **APC: Alternatives, Possibilities and Choices** is a way of taking the blinkers off and looking for other possible actions, solutions, ways of working, explanations etc.
- **OPV: Other Point of View** helps people to consider both sides of a conflict or an argument. What is going through other people's minds? What do they feel?

8. Change the way you see the world

Make your thoughts visible

We were brought up to think with words, but many of the most creative minds in history - novelists, artists and physical scientists - have reported that their most creative inspirations came to them not in words but in visual images. They were able to think with pictures rather than words. Once they got a visual idea, the words were easy. The next time you are faced with a problem, try visualising the solution rather than verbalising it.

Again there are a wide range of tools available to help us think visually and communicate our thoughts visually to others. The collective phrase for these is graphic or visual organisers. They have been around since ancient times, Aristotle used them, so did Leonardo Da Vinci. They have become much more popular recently thanks to Tony Buzan coining the term 'mindmaps' in the 1970's for one form of visual organiser.

Some visual organisers support linear thinking. Others including mindmapping can allow, indeed encourage, thinking which is non linear and outwith or across categories. A simple graphic organiser for young children can be for them to write words randomly on a page to describe a rainy day and draw lines to connect words that can be made into sentences.

Mindmapping allows you to avoid selecting information in categories. This is what Steve Bowkett (1997) calls 'the hardening of the categories'. Instead you can put down the first things that come into your mind and then make associations which are potentially infinite as each association triggers new ones. After you have mindmapped your thoughts, you can look for unifying patterns and connections that might link different thoughts together to form new ideas.

Tony Buzan's classic text on mindmapping has been revised several times and recently he has written books on mindmapping for schools *(see Further Reading)*. Two books on graphic organisers I particularly like are Mapwise (2000) and Eye Cue (2002) by Oliver Caviglioni and Ian Harris. Their approach to mapping and teaching mapping is slightly different from that of Tony Buzan. Several teachers have said to me that they have found the approach to mapping in Mapwise the most straight forward to use with school pupils, and the book Eye Cue lists over forty kinds of graphic organisers. I would also strongly recommend the books of Nancy Margulis (1991) to help pupils draw simple pictures and graphics to illustrate their mindmaps. There is no right way to mindmap but the evidence from teachers suggests that it is better to teach the skill in a systematic way before letting pupils find their own ways of using it.

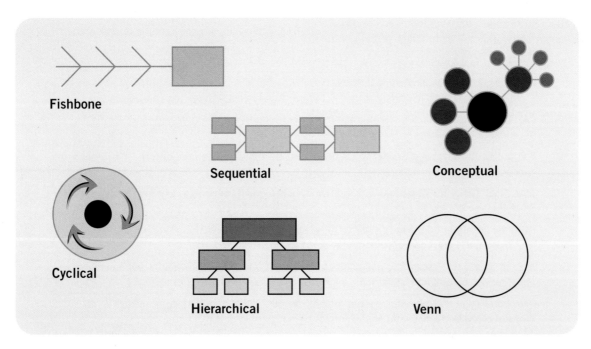

9. Rethink your thinking

"The best way to have a good idea is to have lots of ideas." *Linus Pauling*

Get your thinking out of the box

We often get stuck and can't come up with even one idea. This is a problem because the more ideas we can generate, the better our thinking is likely to be: quantity tends to breed quality. As Foster says, the best way to have an idea is to have an idea. Once we get one idea they tend to snowball. So, to get going, we need one idea, any idea, no matter how senseless it is as long as it is new and different.

The trouble is we weren't taught to think that way. We don't do daft ideas. We've been encouraged to make sense, not nonsense. We have been taught to do this by thinking in a straight line and to work logically through a problem to reach its solution or a conclusion. We have been taught to make sense of the world by classifying and categorising ideas. We are expected to learn facts and be able to recall them. In other words, we have been taught to use what is sometimes called convergent or reproductive thinking. This kind of thinking has its place, but it has a number of limitations, the most important of which is that it doesn't necessarily help us to generate new ideas.

There are other ways of thinking which are sometimes described as divergent or productive thinking which can help anyone to have new ideas. The trouble is they are rarely, if ever, systematically taught in school, despite the fact that, over the last forty years or so, techniques to promote these ways of thinking have been developed. Their foremost inventor is Edward De Bono who created the term lateral thinking as a generic name. He recognised that many of the best ideas arise from mistakes or accidents. The main purpose of lateral thinking is to provide more deliberate ways for pattern switching than relying on a mistake or an accident. De Bono saw lateral thinking as the ability to change perception and keep on changing it. For him, lateral thinking is both an attitude of mind and a number of defined methods.

In lateral or divergent thinking you don't have to follow a logical path. You can take trips down side roads that seem to lead nowhere. You can make jumps; you can start in a completely random place where there may be no road at all; you can even start from a place which is impossible or insane. It can help you avoid assumptions that there are boundaries where there are none. It can help you to avoid restrictions, limitations and constraints which don't actually exist. When you have a problem, it can help you to ask yourself what assumptions you are making that you don't have to make and what unnecessary limits you are setting for yourself.

Silence your internal critic

The rest of this section gives you a very brief insight into divergent thinking techniques and what they can do. None of them will work unless you are willing and able to reserve judgement. When looking for ideas either on your own or with a group, it is essential not to judge, evaluate or criticise ideas as they are being generated. You must silence your internal critic. Otherwise, it's like driving a car with your foot on the accelerator and the brake at the same time.

Look for the best ways to combine hard and soft thinking for you

There are times when lateral or divergent thinking is appropriate and times when it is not. Michalko (2001) has suggested that the secret of deferring judgement is to divide your thinking into two stages: possibility thinking and then practicality thinking. Various people have described the creative process and the different stages in it which can help to think about how and when you can combine hard and soft thinking *(see Focus 2)*. De Bono has also identified a range of thinking hats and suggests a range of orders in which they might be worn, depending on what you are looking for:

9. Rethink your thinking

The six thinking hats

White hat - 'stick to the facts'

Information. Questions. What information do we have? What information do we need to get?

Red hat - 'go with your feelings'

Emotions. Intuition, feelings and hunches. No need to justify feelings. How do I feel about this right now?

Black hat - 'it won't work'

Caution. Judgement. Assessment. Is this true? Will it work? What are the weaknesses? What is wrong with it?

Yellow hat - 'accentuate the positive'

Benefits. Why is this worth doing? What are the benefits? Why can it be done? Why will it work?

Green hat - 'crazy ideas are ok'

Creativity. Different ideas. New ideas. Suggestions and proposals. What are some possible solutions and courses of action? What are the alternatives?

Blue hat - 'let's get the balance right'

Organisation of thinking. Thinking about thinking. How far have we come? What step do we need to take next?

De Bono believes that:

- We all use all of these kinds of thinking, often almost simultaneously, but some of us favour some kinds of thinking more than others
- It helps us to be aware of the kind of thinking we are doing at any point in time
- All kinds of thinking are useful to the effective functioning of a group, but they are best used for different purposes and at different times during a group task

The idea of the six hats is to help us to realise that we don't need to get stuck into using one kind of thinking all the time: we can all use all kinds of thinking depending on what is most useful at the time – it's as easy as taking one hat off and putting another hat on.

Sources: Edward De Bono 'Six Thinking Hats' (1985) and Six Thinking Hats for Schools (1991)

Find ways to 'whack yourself on the side of the head'

This phrase is taken from Roger Von Oech (1990). What follows is a number of techniques recommended by experts for generating out-of-the-box thinking to help you find what you are not looking for. They include making the familiar strange, making novel combinations, coming up with absurd ideas, connecting the unconnected, and looking on the other side. They recognise that the solutions to problems are rational but the ways of finding them may not be.

What ifs

This is a game many advertising agency people play to try to come up with a different way to present the benefits of a product or service. They ask what if we turned the product into something different, for example a person or an animal? What if we made it bigger or smaller? What if we made the service faster or slower? More or less expensive? More or less accessible? The possibilities are endless and the game can also be played to solve a problem. In school, there are all sorts of opportunities for what if questions: what if animals could speak, what if the Germans had won the Second World War etc. It allows the teacher to play devil's advocate with the class.

Provocations

De Bono invented the word 'po' as an abbreviation of provocation in 1968. Provocations take 'what ifs' a stage further. They allow us to make the familiar strange, to escape from normal thought patterns and provide stepping stones to unique solutions or other ways of thinking about a problem or a topic or the world generally. With provocations, we can go mad for thirty seconds at a time in a controlled way and then switch the madness off and on as we wish.

9. Rethink your thinking

According to De Bono, provocations should be bold. There does not need to be any reason for saying something until it is said. In the 'land of po' we can **reverse assumptions**, for example lessons start at 4 o'clock in the afternoon, pupils ask all the questions. We can **exaggerate** so that teachers have six eyes. We can **make the familiar strange** and ask how a teacher is like a tuna sandwich. We can wave a magic wand and **make things disappear.** We can have classrooms with no teachers, doors with no handles and restaurants that don't serve food. We can indulge in **wishful thinking** and have pencils that write by themselves. We can **distort** things and have pupils get their results before they sit the exam. Provocations are not an end in themselves. The idea is to suspend judgement and see if the provocation helps you to move forward to a useful new idea or concept.

Random words

This is a kind of provocation and one of the simplest of all creative techniques. It may seem entirely illogical but can be very powerful. Random words should be nouns. There are lots of ways of obtaining them. For example, think of a page number, then go to that page in a dictionary and find the eighth word down. If that word is not a noun, carry on until you come to the first noun. Link that noun to the problem area you are focusing on and see if it opens up the possibility of new ideas.

Metaphors and analogies

Another way of understanding the familiar by making it strange or of finding unexpected solutions to familiar problems is to use metaphors and analogies.

A metaphor is a descriptive term or phrase given to a person, object or action which is imaginatively but not literally applicable. You can imagine yourself being an object, a kind of food or a kind of animal. You can think of your life as a ball, a battle, a journey or a mission. An analogy is a 'correspondence' or a 'potential similarity'. Drawing analogies is about finding similarities or links between what you are concerned with and want to understand, explain, do, solve or discover and seemingly totally unrelated concepts, ideas, objects, or events. A famous example is George Mestral, the Swiss inventor who developed Velcro by drawing an analogy between the wild burrs he struggled to remove from his dog's coat and a way of fastening millions of different items.

A whole approach to creative problem solving based on using metaphors and analogies has grown out of the work of William Gordon (1961) on Synectics.

9. Rethink your thinking

Focus 4

The Creative Process

We can think of creativity as a linear or a cyclical process which involves a number of steps or stages. Graham Wallas in his book 'The Art of Thought' (1926) was one the first people to attempt to describe the creative process in this way. He saw it as linear and having four stages, namely preparation, incubation, illumination and verification. In 'The Creative Manager', Russell and Evans (1980) added the 'frustration' phase. More recently Mihaly Csikszentmihalyi's 'Creativity' produced the five stages below.

1: Preparation

This is when you become immersed consciously or not in something that takes your interest, arouses your curiosity or is your area of expertise. The stimulus, as it is sometimes called, can be anything – a problem, a perceived need or opportunity, a picture, a story – that creates the possibility of creative ideas.

2: Incubation

This is a time spent away from the problem, usually after actively engaging in it. It is the time to do nothing when too much conscious thinking can get in the way, even get you stuck. During incubation, ideas churn around, are sorted and rearranged often below the threshold of consciousness. During this time, connections are likely to be made, ideas 'call to each other on their own' without any effort to solve the problem consciously and when unexpected combinations may come into being at the oddest moments.

3: Insight or illumination

Sometimes called the 'aha' moment as when Archimedes cried 'Eureka!' as he stepped into the bath and the pieces of the puzzle fell together. Insight can also come slowly and gradually over a long period of time in the way that the theory of the survival of the fittest came to Charles Darwin. It's a mysterious phase that no-one really understands and there are few insights into how to 'help it happen'.

4: Evaluation

This is when you must decide whether the insight is worth pursuing or not. This is often the emotionally trying period when you do not know whether to proceed or not, and when people feel uncertain or insecure. It is when ideas must be sifted to find the most promising one. It's difficult for the best ideas can often be ugly ducklings because they don't appear any good to begin with.

5: Elaboration

Usually, this takes the most time and effort. It is what Edison was referring to when he talked about creativity being 1% inspiration and 99% perspiration. During this period you spend a lot of time refining and improving the idea, the product or the process, producing prototypes or drafting possible solutions or looking for ways to sell or explain it to others.

Health Warning

If taken too literally, these stages or steps can give a seriously distorted picture of the creative process. Many fresh insights can occur during the slog of the elaboration process. It is less linear and more complex, going through many iterative loops. In real life, there may be several moments of significant insight interspersed with periods of preparation, incubation and evaluation. Sometimes incubation can last for years, sometimes it takes a few hours. Sometimes the basic insight emerges slowly, sometimes in a flash. Given all these reservations, this model does offer a relatively appropriate and simple way to organise the complexities involved.

10. Are schools promoting creativity?

> "Children enter school as question marks and leave as periods." *Neil Postman, 1996*

> "This boy shows great originality which must be curbed at all costs." *One of Peter Ustinov's school report cards*

The charge that schools fail to promote creativity is by no means new. Over the last hundred years, a host of well-known educational thinkers and practitioners such as Freobel, Montessori, Steiner, Dewey, Piaget and Bruner have strongly espoused the importance of creativity in education and been critical of school systems for failing to promote it. Several of them set up their own schools which survive on the fringes today.

In section 2, I argued that the need for creativity in the modern world is increasingly recognised by business leaders and politicians as well as educationalists. But as the recognition grows, the education system seems to find it hard to respond, despite all attempts over the past forty years to try to reform it.

Indeed some have argued that a number of reforms in recent years have made the situation worse rather than better. The two government sponsored national reports I cited earlier suggested that many teachers believed this to be the case. What struck the researchers gathering good practice for the 2001 Scottish report on Creativity in Education, and its follow up, 'Creativity Counts' in 2002, was the number of teachers and headteachers who strongly believed that they had achieved their success in promoting creativity despite the school system rather than because of it.

The final report even made a banner headline out of the following statement:

> "Many teachers feel strongly that current priorities and pressures in education inhibit the creative abilities of young people and those who teach them." *Learning and Teaching Scotland, 2001*

Scottish teachers were concerned about greater prescription over what is taught and how it should be taught, and a growing emphasis on coverage of curriculum content, on narrow definitions of achievement, and on assessment for accountability.

As Guy Claxton (1998) says, "There is a wealth of evidence to confirm that when people feel pressurized, judged or stressed, they tend to revert to ways of thinking that are more clear-cut, more tried and tested, more conventional: in a word less creative." He believes this tells us a lot about why so many teachers and their pupils believe they are not creative.

In 'Hare Brain, Tortoise Mind', Claxton suggests that schools simply reflect what society wants. He points out that:

- Our society values cleverness more than wisdom and knowledge more than know-how
- Being clever means using reason and logic; being a quick thinker; having explanations for everything
- Our attitude reflects a deep confusion about knowing and learning
- Contemplation is undervalued: it is less purposeful and clear-cut, more dreamy and messy, but it can tap into the subconscious
- It's associated with wisdom and creativity rather than cleverness

10. Are schools promoting creativity?

It has also led to creativity being pigeonholed and labelled. In many people's minds, it has become associated with the creative arts, thought of as something less important than other subjects or activities that seem to demand what is seen as more conventional academic intelligence. Worst of all, it has come to be associated with an 'anything-goes' kind of approach which has led to a downplaying of the importance of knowledge and skill and a lack of rigour. Though outdated and inaccurate, such views still persist.

Perhaps the view that is most difficult to shift in secondary school is the importance of subject discipline and the dominance of some subjects over others. For some time now, I have challenged secondary teachers in workshops to tell me what are the most important subjects in their school. Immediately a teacher of geography or technology for example will put their hand up to advocate their subject. Politely I tell them I am not interested in what they think the most important subject in the school is but what actually is. In other words, what subjects have the most clout in a secondary school and what subjects the vast majority of their pupils and their parents think are the most important (though they may not be the ones they like the best). Everyone of course comes up with maths and English.

We then go on to construct the 'everyday high school' hierarchy shown below. There may be some disagreements about what levels some subjects slot into but everyone recognises that there is a hierarchy and that personal and social development is at the bottom. My final provocation is to say to them that if secondary schools are not to be thought of as being out of touch with the modern world then PSD needs to be at the top or better still at the centre of what secondary schools are about. In that way they need to be more like primary schools and not vice-versa as has been the trend over the last twenty years.

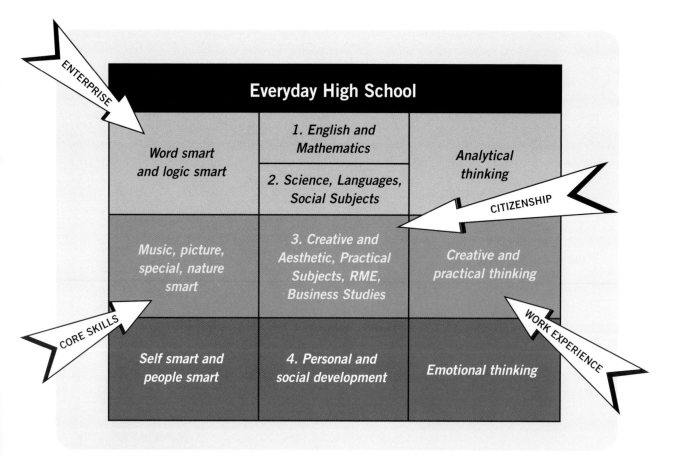

11. The implications for teachers

> "Sometimes the biggest problem with creativity in the classroom is the person in front of it."
>
> *Steven Hastings, 2004*

I've suggested that schools are failing to promote the kind of creative thinking we need in the modern world. In Focus 1, I even talked about school locks on creativity. Now I want to go further and explore the role of classroom teachers in all of this.

Most teaching does not foster creativity

The quote by Stephen Hastings is provocative but not provocative enough for me. I don't think he should have used the word 'sometimes'. I suspect that most teaching does not foster creativity.

I'm not in classrooms regularly enough these days to back this statement up by first hand evidence, but I have spent a great deal of my working life over the past 12 years in deep discussions with thousands of classroom teachers about classroom methodology. On the basis of these discussions, I am willing to bet that if you visit on an average day an average teacher in an average classroom in an average school, you will find the teacher's main purpose is not to foster creativity.

In fact, you will find teachers frowning on the attributes associated with creativity or even doing their best to discourage them. They will emphasise the need for obedience, routine, receptiveness and content coverage rather than the 'could be' attitudes, spontaneity and kinds of thinking I have suggested foster creativity.

Asking pupils to think for themselves and to be more spontaneous is just what many teachers seek to avoid. They suppress spontaneity, stick to routines and try to keep control of their pupils' behaviour and their learning.

Does this mean teachers are to blame?

There are many people around, both educational reformers and politicians, who think teachers are the problem. They are control freaks or are more interested in teaching subjects than fostering young people's creativity.

In my considerable experience of working with teachers, this is simply not true. I firmly believe that the vast majority of teachers want to make a difference of some sort in young people's lives. They buy into the 'dead poets' syndrome to some extent at least. They want to teach their pupils important content and they want them to get good grades. But they also want to help their pupils to enjoy learning and engage with it. They want pupils to think for themselves, make sense of what they are learning and take more responsibility for their own learning. They want their pupils to learn how to learn and become lifelong learners. Arthur Cropley suggests that most primary teachers in particular see developing creativity in young people as one of the key goals of the education system.

Does classroom life undermine creativity?

This begs another question. If many teachers believe they should be fostering creativity then why don't they do it?

Mary Kennedy (2005) has undertaken research into how classroom life can undermine educational reform. Like me, she does not believe it is because teachers do not believe in the thinking and the ideas behind the reforms. Nor does she think that it is mainly because a lot of teachers lack the knowledge, the skills and the confidence to use the strategies that the reforms call for, though she does believe this is an issue.

Her main thesis is that the circumstances of teaching prevent teachers from altering their practice to foster creativity. For her, the daily details of the work of teaching and the structure of the job itself works against what she calls the reform agenda.

11. The implications for teachers

She points out that, in the current system, the teacher's prime responsibility is to make sure that the content of the course is covered and that pupils get through the activities and discussions that are designed to help them learn and ensure that they will perform well in tests and examinations.

This means that the job is very much about maintaining momentum and avoiding distractions. She has found that teachers' fear of distractions is very strong. They don't want to lose their pupils' attention or even worse lose control of their class. As a result, they work hard to create a tranquil environment where pupils feel emotionally safe. This can be hard, especially when there are conflicts between pupils in the class. It is also difficult with a wide range of abilities.

In these circumstances, there is a strong pressure on teachers to suppress spontaneity, to use complex activities which involve intellectual engagement and challenge and even to play down their own enthusiasm. Too much engagement can lead to disruption and open-ended activities heighten the risk of losing sight of the central idea. Active and engaged pupils are more likely to generate ideas that teachers can't anticipate.

Indeed when you ask students to think for themselves, a myriad of ways in which students may deviate from the teacher's envisioned lesson emerge and many of these deviations arise from enthusiasm rather than disengagement. They also arise because pupils are on-task thinking about their learning and trying to make sense of it rather than because they are off-task and trying to disrupt the lesson. Kennedy points out the tension between intellectual engagement and the pressure of time is something that reformers rarely address but teachers must every day of the week. It can leave teachers exhausted and discouraged. That kind of teaching may actually take more time and energy than the majority of teachers actually have.

Is the idea of fostering creativity unrealistic?

Kennedy suggests that the strategies I have been advocating in terms of fostering creativity may simply not be practical for the average teacher, in the average classroom on an average day.

You would not expect me to agree with this but I do agree with the teachers quoted on *page 27* that the current demands of the curriculum and assessment make it very difficult for teachers to foster creativity, wearing them out and undermining their own creativity. We need to make it easier for teachers to foster creativity and give them more practical help to do it.

I'll go on to argue in the last section that we need changes at system level to help schools and teachers to foster creativity, but I do believe that change can also come from the bottom up. The teaching profession needs to influence and lead reform of curriculum and assessment that will make it easier for teachers to employ methodologies which foster young people's creativity rather than stunting it. We can't simply wait until changes happen to us. We need to be proactive and ask ourselves what is possible in our classrooms, now. On *page 31,* I offer some questions for teachers to reflect on together to help them do it.

11. The implications for teachers

Focus 5

Fostering our own creativity

What do we believe about creativity?

What does it mean to us? What relevance does it have to the children we teach and to what we teach? To what extent do we believe it can be fostered?

What status does creativity have in our classrooms?

Do we believe that there are things of inherent value that we should teach irrespective of what's in the exams? Is creativity inherently valuable? If we believe it is, how do we show it? Do we ensure that it is seen as something that requires knowledge, skill and rigour? Do we have high expectations of children in this area?

What kind of atmosphere do we create in our classrooms?

Are we able to create an environment where there is structure and order, where children are challenged and there are high expectations but where children feel safe to come up with ideas and have some measure of freedom to do so?

What mix of teaching methodologies are normally used?

To what extent are children active, engaged and taking responsibility for their own learning? How do we help children to do this and when?

What specific idea getting and idea organising techniques do we use in our teaching and encourage children to use?

Are there some we could use more or different ones we could use? What opportunities are there to use these?

To what extent do we feel we have freedom to improvise?

Do we take opportunities to diverge from the plan on occasions, to improvise and to follow children's interests? What stops us from doing this? How good are we at responding to pupils, unexpected responses? Could we learn techniques to help us do this more effectively and not lose track of our agenda?

Do we feel that 'every minute counts' if we are to cover the curriculum and help children to achieve?

Are we able to give young people the permission and the space to relax and to engage in slow, contemplative thinking? What stops us from doing this?

Are we able to ensure that assessment supports learning and creativity?

Are we able to assess children's creativity in appropriate ways? Are there times when we feel that summative assessment stifles creativity?

What can we actually do to foster our pupils, creativity?

To what extent do we feel 'ground down' by the system and the daily demands of children in the classroom? Do we feel we no longer have the motivation or the energy to devise stimulating activities and to challenge young people's thinking? Are we tempted at times to simply react and give up, cover the ground and teach to the test? Are there small changes we could make to our practice that would make learning more stimulating and enjoyable for our pupils and teaching more stimulating and enjoyable for us?

What do we do to maintain and develop our own creativity?

The most important question and crucially linked to the last one. It applies not just to life in the school and classroom but to life generally.

12. The implications for school leadership

As I pointed out in section 3 and will return to in section 13, there are major implications for the school system, especially the secondary school system in what we have been discussing.

A great deal has been written on the leadership of management and creativity. Kao says that it is rich in paradoxes. Managers must control without controlling and direct without directing. They can't demand creativity any more than they can order growth from a flower. John Grant notes that innovation thrives in free-ranging working conditions. People who are constrained by bureaucracy, convention or oppressive supervision tend to behave in stereotypical rather than innovative ways.

In this section, I shall confine myself to three questions that school leaders who have to make the best of the present system might ask themselves in connection with fostering creativity in both staff and students.

In what ways are you yourself innovative?

Henry Drucker (1993) believes we are all capable of being innovative as individuals, but he doesn't think governments are good at it. He believes the best innovation is found 'way down and close to events'. For him, innovation is not primarily about generating new ideas but about recognising good ideas that are already around and putting them into practice through ingenuity and hard work. He also thinks that although innovation is risky, successful innovations are not mainly about taking risks but seizing opportunities that arise. This is an interesting observation for people working in a profession not renowned for risk-taking!

How do you support and encourage teachers to be energy creators?

Just as good teachers foster creativity in their pupils, so good schools foster creativity in their teachers so that they become energy creators. Jennifer James (1996) points out that many teachers entering the traditional classroom take all the energy out of it. Some people walk into a room and the energy level goes up. Others walk into a room and the energy level drops.

Tim Brighouse and Peter Woods (1999) suggest that "All children are full of 'e' in all its forms – energy, excitement, enthusiasm, effort, effervescence and enterprise. The trick is to release that 'e'. The more teachers can match these personal 'e' factors the more successful they will be and the more fun they will be." The challenge for teachers in the modern classroom is how to exploit the 'e' factors, while still maintaining control. It is no longer possible to motivate pupils by simply extinguishing the 'e' factors.

Kennedy (2005) describes the impossible tension between stimulating pupils to think and the everyday reality of being a teacher in a system which demands content coverage, expects teachers to deal with disruptive children in the classroom and also teach classes with a wide range of ability levels. She also points out that the school itself can create the constant interruptions that are one of the biggest challenges for teachers.

If they are to help teachers to be energy creators, schools need to look at their policies on major issues such as inclusion, mixed ability classes and also what are considered minor issues such as interruption of classroom lessons.

Are you open to the idea of fewer lessons and more projects that relate to the real world?

Being creative helps us to solve problems, evaluate options and take decisions on a daily basis in the real world. The problem is that most everyday problems are not like the ones that have been traditionally set in school.

11. The implications for school leadership

In school...	In everyday life...
• Problems are chosen for you and given to you	• Problems just arise: you have to recognise that they are problems
• You are told what the nature of the problem is	• You have to work out what the nature of the problem is
• Problems are structured: there are steps you have to go through to solve them	• Problems are messy: they cannot be solved in ten easy steps
• You are given the information you need to solve the problem	• It's not clear what information you will need to solve the problem and it might not be available
• Problems are usually taken out of context	• Problems depend on the context: they repeatedly confront us with 'it depends'
• Problems usually have a right answer	• Problems generally have no one right answer
• They are usually tackled by individuals	• They are usually tackled in groups

John Holt (1964) showed that, from the learner's point of view, most lessons seem meaningless. They consist of a series of tasks to get through and be rid of. Projects can provide something different and more meaningful if:

- They are designed to produce a product, for a purpose and an audience
- The audience is as 'real-world' as possible and the purpose and product authentic
- The activity is challenging and requires a wide range of skills
- The activity requires learners to participate and work with each other
- The learners are given responsibility to make important decisions
- The task demands the use of real resources that need to be sought out or created
- The activity takes time to complete, requires careful planning and entails making some mistakes
- Help and support is needed from adults who act as mentors
- Learners get feedback on process as well as product
- Success is celebrated on completion of the activity

David Hargreaves (2004) claims that our current problem is that projects have been squeezed out of secondary schools because of the need to cover ground and prepare for examinations and have been given a bad name in primary schools because they were unfocussed and lacked the kinds of features identified above. He suggests that they need to be rehabilitated rather than abandoned.

There are some very promising initiatives around which can help teachers and schools to develop more collaborative, more project based and more creative approaches to learning and teaching. Two outstanding examples are the work being undertaken by the RSA 'Open Minds' initiative and the Critical Skills Programme, a division of Network Educational Press Limited *(see References)*.

13. The implications for educational reform

Be clearer about what is important

David Perkins (date) suggested that what we want from our schools is 'everything'. Everyone, including teachers, reformers, parents and politicians, have many ideas about what they want schools to do and sometimes they conflict with one another. We want youngsters to learn specific content, we want them to get good grades, we want them to be nurtured and develop into good citizens. When a problem arises in our society, we add things into the school curriculum and hardly anything drops out.

The one reform objective that virtually everyone says they want and no politician could openly argue with is inclusion. We want all our children to be happy and to 'be all they can be'. We believe this means they all should have an equal chance to succeed at school and have access to the very best teaching to help to do so.

But the question we don't ask often enough is what we mean by success and even happiness. Other countries, like Norway for instance, have been better at this. Recently however, Scotland has taken a big step forward in this regard in a policy paper entitled, 'A Curriculum for Excellence 3-18' which lists the qualities we want young people to have so that long after school they will be responsible citizens, effective contributors, successful learners and confident individuals. It is the first time we have had a statement of what we consider to be important that everyone can rally round. But, if we are serious about this list, it has huge implications for what we do in schools.

> "The curriculum should not be thought of as a course to run but as a network of important ideas to explore."
>
> *Richard Prawat*

De-clutter the curriculum

We need to teach less but teach it better. We need more depth and less breadth. In too many countries, the curriculum is a mile wide and an inch deep. We have seen that when teachers are asked to cover too much ground, the temptation is to keep the momentum of the lesson going and to avoid asking questions or devising activities that encourage lateral thinking.

'A Curriculum for Excellence' has called for a 'significant decluttering' of the primary curriculum in Scotland and groups are already looking at the secondary curriculum. It suggests that the curriculum must make learning active, challenging and enjoyable and should not be too fragmented or over-crowded with content. Perhaps we are finally coming to the view of Richard Prawat (1992).

See teachers as the solution rather than the problem

Kennedy's fascinating research inside classrooms should give all those involved in educational reform pause to think about why a lot of educational reform does not happen in the classroom. Often we see classroom teachers as blocks to change and dismiss their protestations about how hard it is to change classroom practice as at best excuses and at worst sabotage. No reform can happen unless classroom teachers not only go along with it but lead it. We must ensure that they not only have the freedom to foster creativity in the classroom but that they have the energy and the skill to do it. Without that, nothing that has been discussed here will become a reality.

References

1. A Curriculum for Excellence, Scottish Executive, 2005.
2. All Our Futures: Creativity, Culture and Education: Report from the National Advisory Committee on Creative and Cultural Education, May 1999.
3. Ambitious Excellent Schools, Scottish Executive, 2005.
4. Brighouse, Tim and Woods, Peter, 'How to Improve Your School', Routledge, London, 1999.
5. Claxton, Guy, 'The Wayward Mind', Little and Brown, London, 2005.
6. Cropley, Arthur, 'Creativity in Education and Learning', Kogan Page, London, 2001.
7. Csikszentmihalyi, Mihaly, 'Creativity: Flow and the Psychology of Discovery and Invention', Harper Collins, 1996.
8. Damasio, Antonio, 'Some notes on the Brain, Imagination and Creativity' in Karl Pfenninger, 'The Origins of Creativity', Oxford, 2001.
9. De Bono, Edward, 'Po: Getting Beyond Yes and No', Penguin, New York, 1972.
10. Drucker, Henry, 'Innovation and Entrepreneurship', Harper Business, New York, 1993.
11. Giddens, Anthony, 'Runaway World', Routledge, New York, 2003.
12. Dryden, Windy, 'Overcoming Guilt', Sheldon Press, London, 1994.
13. Gordon, William, 'Synectics: the Development of Creative Capacity', New York, 1961.
14. Greenspan, Stanley, 'The Growth of the Mind', Addison-Wesley, Massachusetts, 1997.
15. Grant, John, 'Seven Steps to Creativity', in 'Changing Behaviours', The Design Council, 2001.
16. Hargreaves, David, 'Towards Education for Innovation', in 'Changing Behaviours', The Design Council, 2001.
17. Hastings, Steven, Creativity article in TES February 27 2004.
18. Holt, John, 'How Children Fail', Pelican, Middlesex, 1964.
19. James, Jennifer, 'Thinking in the Future Tense', Simon and Schuster, New York, 1996.
20. John-Steiner, Vera, 'Creative Collaboration', OUP, 2000.
21. Johnstone, Keith, 'Impro: Improvisation and the Theatre', Methuen, 1981.
22. Kao, John, 'Jamming: The Art and Discipline of Business Creativity', Harper Collins, London, 1997.
23. Kennedy, Mary, 'Inside Teaching: How Classroom Life Undermines Reform', Harvard College, 2005.
24. Koestler, Arthur, 'The Act of Creation', Penguin, London, 1964.
25. Land, George and Jarman, Beth 'Breakpoint and Beyond', Harper Business, New York, 1992.
26. Learning and Teaching Scotland, 'Creativity in Education', Dundee, 2001.
27. Learning and Teaching Scotland, 'Creativity Counts', Dundee, 2002.
28. Maslow, Abraham, 'Emotional Blacks to Creativity', lecture 1957 (cited in Land and Jarman).
29. Maxwell, James Clerk: for a biography see www.studyworld.com/james_clark_maxwell.htm.
30. Mead, Margaret, 'Culture and Commitment', Anchor Books, 1970.
31. Morgan, Lloyd, 'A History of Psychology', 1930.
32. Myers, David, 'Psychology', Worth Publishers, New York, 1995.
33. Piaget, Jean, 'The Child's Conception of the World', 1926.
34. Pinker, Steven, 'The Blank Slate', Penguin Books, London, 2002.
35. Postman, Neil, 'The End of Education', Vintage Books, New York, 1996.
36. Prawat, Richard, 'Teachers' Beliefs about Teaching and Learning', in The American Journal of Education, 1992.
37. Rothenberg, Albert, 'Creativity and Madness', John Hopkins, Baltimore and London, 1990.
38. Russell, Peter and Evans, Roger, 'The Creative Manager', New York, 1992.
39. Wallas, Graham, 'The Art of Thought' 1926.
40. Waugh, Alison, 'Thinking and Creativity', a presentation for NESTA, 10 July 2003 available at www.nesta.com.

further reading

Further reading

1. Bowkett, Stephen, 'Imagine That', Network Educational Press, Stafford, 1997.
2. Bowkett, Stephen, 'Self-Intelligence', Network Educational Press, Stafford 1999.
3. Bromley, Karen et al, 'Graphic Organisers', Scholastic Press, New York, 1995.
4. Buzan, Tony and Barry, 'The Mind Map Book', BBC, London 2003.
5. Buzan, Tony, 'Brain Child', Harper Collins, London, 2003.
6. Cameron, Julia, 'The Artist's Way', Pan Books, London, 1994.
7. Caviglioni, Oliver and Harris, Ian, 'Mapwise', Network Educational Press, Stafford, 2000.
8. Caviglioni, Oliver, Harris, Ian and Tindall, Bill, 'Eye Cue', Network Educational Press, Stafford, 2002.
9. Csikszentmihalyi, Mihaly, 'Flow: The Psychology of Human Happiness' Random Century Group, London, 1992.
10. Claxton, Guy, 'Hare Brain Tortoise Mind: why intelligence increases when you think less', Fourth Estate, London, 1998.
11. Claxton, Guy and Lucas, Bill, 'Be Creative', BBC Books, London, 2004.
12. De Bono, Edward, 'Lateral Thinking', Penguin, London, 1970.
13. De Bono, Edward, 'Six Thinking Hats', Penguin, London, 1985.
14. De Bono, Edward, 'Six Thinking Hats for Schools', Perfection Learning Corporation, 1991.
15. De Bono, Edward, 'Serious Creativity', Harper Collins, London, 1992.
16. De Bono, Edward, 'Teach Your Child to Think', Penguin, London, 1992.
17. De Bono, Edward, 'De Bono's Thinking Course', BBC Books, London, 1994.
18. Fisher, Robert, 'Teaching Children to Think', Simon and Schuster, 1990.
19. Foster, Jack, 'How to Get Ideas', Beret-Koehler, San Francisco, 1996.
20. Giddens, Anthony, 'Runaway World', Profile Books Limited, 2002.
21. Hargreaves, Andy, 'Teaching in the Knowledge Society', OUP, Maidenhead, 2003.
22. Hargreaves, David, 'Learning for Life', The Policy Press, Bristol, 2004.
23. Margulis, Nancy, 'Mapping Inner Space', Zephyr Press, Tucson Arizona, 1991.
24. Michalko, Michael, 'Cracking Creativity', Ten Speed Press, California, 2001.
25. Robinson, Ken, 'Out of Our Minds: Learning to be Creative', Capstone Limited, Oxford, 2001.
26. Von Oech, Roger, 'A Whack on the Side of the Head', Thorsons, Wellingborough, 1990.
27. Von Oech, Roger, 'Expect the Unexpected', The Free Press, New York, 2001.
28. Wiseman, Robert, 'Did You Spot the Gorilla?', Arrow Books, London, 2004.

Websites

1. www.creativitycentre.com
2. www.ncaction.org.uk/creativity/index.htm
3. www.thersa.org
4. www.capeuk.org
5. www.creativepartnerships.com
6. www.nfer.ac.uk/research/arts.asp
7. www.criticalskills.co.uk